CONTENTS

labor costs and increase productivity

YES YOU CAN

How Millennial's Can Build Wealth Over Time

Kaitlin Henderson

Copyright

Except as permitted by Sections 107 or 108 of the 1976 United States Copyright Act, no part of this publication may be duplicated, stored in a retrieval system, or transmitted in any form or by any means, electronic, mechanical, photocopying, recording, scanning, or otherwise, without the prior written consent of the Publisher.

Copyright © 2023 By Kaitlin Henderson

INTRODUCTION

The truth is that Millennial's, often known as Generation Y, suffer particular difficulties in accumulating wealth. Millennial's are sometimes accused of being financially irresponsible. Many people have a high cost of living, minimal job security, and heavy student loan debt. But Millennial's can still attain financial independence and wealth with the appropriate approaches and outlook.

Adopting the idea of "becoming rich slowly" is a crucial technique for Millennial's to amass wealth. This entails investing for the long term and accumulating wealth instead of looking for fast money through hazardous bets or get-rich-quick scams. Millennial's can build wealth and achieve financial freedom by making wise financial decisions and investing consistently.

Prioritizing saving is the first step in building wealth gradually. This is living within your means and setting aside a certain amount of money each month for savings. But saving a minuscule 20% of your salary is ideal; even just 10% of your income can add up over time. Budget and track your expenses to find areas where you may reduce wasteful spending.

Investing is a crucial component of wealth accumulation. Even if you're new to investing, this can seem unsafe, but it's vital for long-term financial success. Via a retirement plan like a 401(k) or IRA, Millennial's can begin saving in one of the simplest ways possible. These accounts make it simple to save money and invest since they provide tax benefits and allow automatic deductions from your salary.

Millennial's can consider investing in low-cost exchange-traded funds or index funds in addition to retirement accounts (ETFs). These funds can deliver consistent returns over time and provide exposure to various stocks or bonds. Remember that investing entails some risk, but you can lower your risk and improve your chances of success by investing consistently and diversifying your portfolio.

Millennial's might think about strategies to enhance their income in addition to saving and investing. This can entail looking for a job that pays more or beginning a side business. Your progress toward financial independence will be sped up by raising your income, allowing you to save and invest more.

Thirdly, Millennial's should adopt a long-term perspective when accumulating wealth. Becoming wealthy gradually is a process that takes time and requires endurance rather than a quick fix. You can achieve financial freedom and earn money that will last a lifetime by concentrating on your long-term objectives and making steady progress over time.

In conclusion, even if Millennial's have particular difficulties creating money, it is still possible for them to reach financial independence and even fortune. Millennial's can accumulate wealth and achieve financial independence by gradually getting rich, emphasizing saving and investing, growing their income, and developing a long-term perspective. The future is promising for this generation, and they may anticipate a lifetime of financial freedom and security provided they adopt the appropriate techniques and mindset.

CHAPTER 1: BEING AWARE OF HOW IMPORTANT INVESTING AND SAVING ARE FOR BUILDING LONG-TERM WEALTH.

For Millennial's, saving and investing are two essential parts of accumulating long-term wealth. But it might be challenging to know where to begin, particularly if you're just starting on your financial path. This article will discuss the value of saving and investing and offer practical advice to get you started.

How Crucial Is Saving?

Setting away money for future use is the act of saving. By saving, you can create a financial safety net and prepare for unforeseen costs. Also, it aids in achieving long-term financial objectives, including home ownership, business startup, and comfortable retirement.

Compound interest has the potential to be one of the saving's most important advantages. The interest earned on the initial investment plus any additional interest is compound. This may cause your funds to rise significantly over time. For instance, if you invested $1,000 now and received 5% interest annually, you would have $1,628.89 after ten years. This is so that your money can expand exponentially over time because the claim you make on your initial investment is reinvested.

Savings also aids in debt avoidance. When you have savings, you're less likely to use loans or credit cards to cover unforeseen costs. Doing this can decrease debt with high-interest rates and raise your credit score.

Save Money

Setting up a budget is the first step toward saving money. A budget is a plan that outlines how you will divide your money between savings and expenses. While making your budget, it's critical to be practical and set aside adequate money for savings. Generally, aim to save at least 20% of your income.

Create an emergency fund next. A savings account known as an emergency fund can be used to pay for unforeseen expenses like a car repair or medical emergency. Your emergency fund should contain three to six months of living expenses.

Lastly, take into account automating your savings. Setting up automatic transfers from your checking account to your savings account will enable you to accomplish this. By doing this, you can be confident that you're continually conserving money and remove any desire to spend it elsewhere.

How Crucial Is Investing?

While saving is substantial, investing is crucial for building long-term wealth. To make a return, investing entails putting your money to work in the stock market, real estate, or other assets.

Compound interest accrues as you invest, which has the potential to increase your funds significantly. The stock market has previously offered investors an average annual return of about 10%. This has the potential to generate significant wealth accumulation over time.

You may diversify your portfolio and lower risk by investing, too. You can reduce your exposure to the dangers of any one investment by diversifying your holdings.

What To Invest In

Establishing your investment objectives and risk tolerance is the first stage in the investing process. Your investment objectives will dictate how much money you need to put aside and the kinds of assets you should consider. How much risk you will take to meet your investment objectives will depend on your risk tolerance.

After then, think about your investing possibilities. Investments come in various forms, including stocks, bonds, mutual funds, and real estate. Research is essential before investing because every investment type has advantages and risks.

Consider consulting a financial professional or hiring a robo-advisor once you've chosen your investment strategy. A financial advisor can assist you in developing a customized investment strategy and offer continuing advice and support. An automated investment platform, a robo-advisor employs algorithms to manage your investments on your goals and risk tolerance.

Conclusion

Building long-term wealth and achieving financial freedom need both saving and investment. While investing enables you to benefit from compound interest and increase your wealth over time, saving lays the groundwork for long-term financial security.

As a millennial, it's crucial to start investing and saving early to benefit from compound interest. You may begin saving consistently and laying a solid basis for your financial future by creating a budget, setting up an emergency fund, and automating your savings.

Studying and comprehending your financial possibilities when it comes to investing is crucial. Consider working with a robo-advisor or financial professional to help you develop a customized investment strategy and reduce risk.

The secret to steadily becoming wealthy as a millennial is prioritizing saving and investing while being dedicated to your long-term financial objectives. You may attain financial independence and accumulate long-term wealth with perseverance, self-control, and basic financial literacy.

CHAPTER 2: SECTORS AND CAREER PATHWAYS WITH HIGH EARNINGS POTENTIAL FOR MILLENNIAL'S.

Finding sectors and career paths with high earning potential as a millennial is crucial for reaching financial independence and creating lasting wealth. Finding the right area to concentrate on can take time because of how quickly the economy changes and develops.

In this chapter, we'll examine the top professions and industries for Millennial's in terms of income potential and offer advice on how to set yourself up for success in each of these areas.

1. Technology

1. Technology   The top five highest-paying positions in technology, according to Glassdoor, are enterprise architect, software engineering manager, software development manager, director of engineering, and program manager.
Building a solid network, staying current with emerging trends and technologies, and consistently honing your abilities are

essential for success in the technology sector.

2. Healthcare

A combination of an aging population and rising demand for healthcare services fuel tremendous expansion in the healthcare sector. According to Forbes, the top five highest-paying positions in the healthcare industry are surgeon, psychiatrist, physician, orthodontist, and dentist.

You'll need to finish rigorous education and training, stay current on the most recent medical advancements, and develop strong communication and interpersonal skills to flourish in the healthcare sector.

3. Banking

According to Glassdoor, the top five financial positions in terms of pay are: Tax Director, Portfolio Manager, Enterprise Architect, Director of Operations
You'll need strong quantitative and analytical abilities, outstanding communication skills, and a thorough knowledge of financial markets and trends to succeed in finance.

4. Law

The legal sector, which includes lawyers, judges, and corporate counsel, offers some of the highest-paying positions. According to Glassdoor, the top five legal positions with the highest salaries are general counsel, attorney, law clerk, associate attorney, and paralegal.
A law degree, solid analytical and research skills, and good communication and negotiation abilities are all prerequisites for success in the legal field.

5. Engineering

Electrical, civil, and mechanical engineering are among the high-paying professions in the engineering sector. According to Glassdoor, the top five engineering positions with the highest salaries are Enterprise Architect, Director of Engineering, Director of Operations, Director of Strategy, and Systems Architect.

You'll need strong analytical and problem-solving abilities, outstanding communication skills, and a thorough understanding of engineering concepts and technology to thrive in engineering.

How To Set Yourself Up For Success

After determining the industries and career options with the most earning potential, setting yourself up for success is critical. Here are some pointers to get you going:

1. Improve your abilities

It's crucial to continuously improve your abilities and keep up with the newest trends and technologies to excel in any business. Consider taking classes, attending conferences, and earning certifications to enhance your skills and expertise.

2. Create a robust network

Finding jobs, obtaining recommendations, and understanding industry trends depend on a good network. To expand your network, go to industry events, sign up for groups for professionals, and connect with them on LinkedIn.

3. Acquire knowledge

Getting experience through internships, volunteer work, or freelance projects is crucial to stand out in a crowded employment market. You may use this to improve your talents, create a portfolio, and show prospective employers how valuable you are.

4. Act decisively

In your career, being proactive and taking the initiative are crucial. This entails actively looking for possibilities, networking, feedback, and mentorship from more seasoned experts in your sector.

5. Contemplate pursuing a degree.

A master's degree or an advanced certification might open up more professional growth chances and higher-paying positions in some industries. Consider the return on investment to decide whether investing in more education is worthwhile for your job ambitions.

Conclusion

Finding industries and career paths with high earning potential is a crucial first step for Millennial's who want to become financially independent and amass lasting wealth. You may set yourself up for success in these high-paying sectors by concentrating on industries like technology, healthcare, finance, law, and engineering, obtaining the essential abilities, building a solid network, earning experience, and exercising initiative. Remember that reaching financial success requires perseverance, hard effort, and a long-term outlook. Still, with the appropriate plan, you can accomplish your objectives and create your desired financial future.

CHAPTER 3: ESTABLISHING AND ADHERING TO A BUDGET TO MANAGE TO SPEND

Making and following a budget are two crucial elements in gaining financial independence. A budget is a financial strategy that helps you manage your money by outlining your income and expenses. You may find out where you're overspending, make changes to limit the costs, and save money by making a budget.

In this chapter, we'll go through how to make a budget and offer advice on how to stick to it.

Step 1: Determine Your Income

Determining your income is the first step in making a budget. Any sources of income, such as your salary, bonuses, or freelancing, are included in this. For a complete view of your financial condition, be sure to include all sources of income.

Step 2: Determine Your Fixed Costs

Determine your fixed expenses as the next stage. These include costs like rent, mortgage payments, auto payments, and insurance premiums that don't change from month to month. Make careful to account for fixed expenses in your budget since they are usually simpler to predict since they are constant.

Step 3: Determine Your Variable Costs

Expenses vary from month to month for groceries, entertainment, and apparel. Track your expenditures for a month or two to observe where your money will determine your variable expenses. This will assist you in making a more precise budget and locating areas where you can reduce expenditure.

Step 4. Establish financial goals

Establishing financial objectives is a crucial stage in developing a budget. Decide on your financial goals, such as debt repayment, home down payment savings, or emergency fund development. Setting financial objectives will give you a specific aim, which can keep you motivated and concentrated.

Step 5: Distribute the Money

Allocating funds comes after figuring out your income, fixed and variable expenses, and financial objectives. Then, give the remaining cash to your variable expenses after paying for your set expenses and financial goals. Make sure to budget extra money in case of unforeseen costs or emergencies.

Guidelines For Maintaining Your Budget

Budgeting is one thing, but following it is another. The following advice will assist you in controlling spending and adhering to your budget:

1. Monitor Your Expenditures

Maintaining your budget requires tracking your spending. Track your spending with a spreadsheet or budgeting tool and make adjustments as necessary. You'll gain a better knowledge of where your money is going and be able to make wise decisions about your spending if you keep track of your expenditures.

2. Resist making rash purchases

Impulsive purchases can easily throw your budget off course. Please make a list before shopping and stick to it to prevent impulse buys. If you see something you like but not on your list, wait a few days to decide if you need it before buying.

3. Search for ways to reduce your spending

Find strategies to reduce spending without compromising your quality of life. Consider eating less out and cooking more at home, or giving up cable and switching to streaming services. You can save money over time by making several minor adjustments.

4. Pay with cash rather than credit.

You may better manage your expenditures and prevent overspending by paying with cash instead of credit. Use a predetermined amount each week or month to cover your variable expenses. You'll have to wait until the following week or month to make more purchases when the money is spent.

5. Remain Motivated

Finally, maintain motivation by concentrating on your financial objectives. Keep track of your development and honor minor accomplishments along the way. If you remain motivated, you'll be more likely to stick to your spending plan and reach your financial objectives.

Conclusion

Controlling spending and gaining financial independence

requires developing and adhering to a budget. You can make a budget that works for you by determining your income, fixed and variable expenses, financial objectives, and allocating monies. Track your spending, refrain from impulsive purchases, seek ways to reduce costs, pay with cash instead of credit, and maintain your motivation to reach your financial objectives. You can successfully manage your finances, keep costs under control, and create the financial future you want if you are dedicated and disciplined.

CHAPTER 4: ESTABLISHING AN EMERGENCY FUND TO PREVENT FINANCIAL SETBACKS

Despite your best efforts to plan, unforeseen costs might still occur at any time, resulting in a loss of funds. Building an emergency fund is one of the best methods to shield yourself from financial shocks. A savings account for unforeseen costs like medical bills, auto repairs, or job loss is known as an emergency fund. This post will discuss the value of creating an emergency fund and offer advice on where to begin.

What Makes An Emergency Fund Important?

You require an emergency fund for several reasons. First, unanticipated costs can arise anytime, regardless of how well you prepare. If you don't have emergency savings, you could use credit cards or loans to pay the bills, resulting in debt and financial hardship.

Second, peace of mind can be obtained from having an emergency fund. Knowing that you have money for unforeseen costs might be reassuring, increasing your sense of security and self-assurance.

An emergency fund can also prevent you from using other funds, such as in your retirement account or down payment money. You can protect your additional funds and prevent them from being depleted in the event of an unforeseen need by setting aside a separate account for emergencies.

How To Create A Disaster Fund

Though it may seem complicated, creating an emergency fund is essential to achieving financial security. Here are some pointers to get you going:

1. Establish Your Goal Amount

Choosing how much to save is the first step in creating an emergency fund. Aim for three to six months' living expenses as a general guideline. If you lose your job or incur another unforeseen cost, this should be sufficient to pay your expenses. You want to aim for a more excellent emergency fund if your income is higher or your work is more erratic.

2. Create a unique savings account

Create a separate savings account for your emergency fund once you've decided on your target amount. Emergency access to this account should be simple and different from other savings accounts. To help your money increase over time, find a savings account with a high-interest rate.

3. Begin modestly and expand gradually

Don't feel you have to save your desired amount simultaneously because creating an emergency fund can take time. Start small and expand progressively. Weekly sums of $25 or $50 might pile up over time to help you attain your goal.

4. Reduce Costs and Boost Income

Look for strategies to boost your income and decrease spending to help you save more money rapidly. Put less money into your emergency fund by cutting back on non-essential costs like eating out or subscription services. You can also try to find ways to get more money, including getting a second job or requesting a pay raise at work.

5. Automatically Save Money

One of the most straightforward strategies to accumulate an emergency fund is automating your savings. Create a scheduled transfer from your checking account to your savings account for an emergency fund each month. If you do it this way, you won't have to remember to save each month, and your savings will increase over time.

Conclusion

The first step in achieving financial security and preventing financial setbacks is saving for emergencies. You may create an emergency fund that gives you peace of mind and protects you from unforeseen expenses by deciding on your target amount, setting up a separate savings account, starting small and developing over time, lowering expenses and boosting income, and automating your savings. Remember that creating an emergency fund requires patience and discipline, but the rewards—financial security and peace of mind—make an effort worthwhile.

CHAPTER 5: MAKING DEBT REPAYMENT A TOP PRIORITY TO LOWER INTEREST COSTS AND RAISE CREDIT SCORES

Financial stress can be significantly increased by debt, which, if not controlled, can quickly mount up and become impossible to handle. Debt affects your finances and may also negatively impact your credit score, making it more challenging to get credit or loans. This post will discuss the significance of prioritizing debt repayment and offer advice on lowering interest costs and raising your credit score.

Why Paying Down Debt Should Be Your First Priority

For several reasons, paying off debt should be a high priority in your financial plan. The first benefit of paying off debt is that it lowers the total amount you owe and releases cash flow for other needs, like savings or investments.

Second, setting debt repayment as a top priority might result in long-term financial savings. You pay more interest fees the longer you carry a debt. Over time, you can save hundreds or thousands of dollars in interest by making your debts as quickly as possible.

Finally, setting debt repayment as a top priority can help you raise your credit score. Your payment history, credit utilization, and length of credit history are just a few variables that determine your credit score. You can raise your credit score and increase your chances of getting credit or loans by making on-time debt payments and lowering your credit use.

Advice For Setting Debt Repayment Priorities

The following advice can help you prioritize paying off debt and cutting interest costs:

1. List your obligations and interest rates.

Identifying your obligations and their interest rates is the first step in prioritizing debt repayment. This will assist you in choosing which bills to pay off first. Please include all of your debts, including loans, credit cards, and other types of debt, along with their associated interest rates.

2. Prioritize high-interest debt

Focus on paying off the loan with the highest interest rate first after you have listed your debts and their rates. In the long run, you will be able to save money by lowering the number of interest charges you pay.

3. Think about debt consolidation

Consider merging multiple high-interest debts into a single loan or credit card with a lower interest rate if you have many high-interest bills. This can lower your interest costs and make your debt repayment plan simpler.

4. Pay more than the required amount

Aim to pay more than the minimum amount each month to pay off debt as rapidly as feasible. You can reduce the interest you pay on your debt by paying an extra $25 or $50 each month.

5. Seek For Ways to Raise More Money

Look for strategies to enhance your income to assist you in paying off your debt more rapidly. Think about getting a side job, doing freelance work, reselling your old belongings, or asking for a raise at work.

6. Avoid taking on new debt

Refraining from acquiring new debt while paying off existing debt is crucial. This can be difficult, but it's essential to keeping up your success and preventing further financial strain.

Conclusion

To achieve financial security and lessen financial stress, it is crucial to prioritize debt repayment. You can pay off your debt more quickly, save money on interest payments, and raise your credit score by identifying your deficits and interest rates, concentrating on the high-interest debt first, consolidating debt, paying more than the minimum, looking for ways to increase your income, and avoiding taking on new debt. Remember that paying off debt requires patience and discipline, but the rewards—financial security and peace of mind—are worth the effort.

CHAPTER 6: SELECTING THE CORRECT RETIREMENT ACCOUNT TYPE AND MAKING REGULAR CONTRIBUTIONS

Although retirement may seem far off, there is always time to begin preparations. Making the appropriate retirement account selections and regular contributions is essential to guarantee you will have enough money to sustain yourself in retirement. In this post, we'll look at the various retirement account types and offer advice on how to pick the best one and make regular contributions.

Retirement Account Types

There are various retirement accounts kinds, each with unique features and advantages. The most typical types of retirement accounts are listed below:

1. Plan 401 (k)

401(k) plans are employer-sponsored retirement accounts that permit employees to make pre-tax contributions to the budget for a portion of their salary. 401(k) plans are a popular option for retirement savings since many businesses provide matching contributions.

2. Conventional IRA

Traditional IRAs are individual retirement accounts that let you make pre-tax contributions deductible from taxes and grow tax-deferred until retirement. The maximum annual contribution is $6,000 (or $7,000 if you're 50 or older).

3. The Roth IRA

Another kind of individual retirement plan that enables after-tax contributions is the Roth IRA. While donations are not tax-deductible, they provide tax-free growth and tax-free withdrawals in retirement.

4. SEP IRA

A Simplified Employee Pension (SEP) IRA is a retirement account for self-employed people or small business owners. You are permitted to contribute up to $58,000, or up to 25% of your net profits (as of 2021).

Selecting The Correct Retirement Account Type

Your best retirement account type will depend on several variables, including your age, income, and employment. Here are some pointers to help you choose the best retirement account:

1. Examine the plan of your employer
It's typically a good idea to contribute to your employer's 401(k) plan if available, especially if your employer matches your

contribution. Nonetheless, you might think about opening an IRA or SEP IRA if your employer doesn't have a retirement plan or if you work for yourself.

2. Consider Your Tax Status
A regular IRA or 401(k) may be wise if your current tax bracket is greater than the one you anticipate having in retirement. On the other hand, a Roth IRA might be a better option if you anticipate being in a higher tax bracket in retirement because you'll pay taxes on your contributions now rather than when you're older.

3. Examine Your Retirement Objectives
Your retirement objectives should influence your choice of retirement account. A Roth IRA might be a wise decision if you're starting to save for retirement early and want to get the most out of your money because it allows your contributions to grow tax-free for an extended period.

4. Participating Often

The correct retirement account type is only half the battle; you must also make regular contributions to maximize your retirement savings. Here are some pointers for consistently contributing:

1. Configure automatic donations
You may easily ensure that you're making regular contributions to your retirement account by setting up automatic contributions. Either your bank or the retirement plan offered by your Company allows you to set up automatic contributions.

2. Gradually increase your contributions
Start modest and gradually increase your payments to your retirement account if you cannot immediately contribute the maximum amount. Over time, even modest contributions might add up.

3. Use catch-up contributions to your advantage

You may increase your annual retirement account contributions if you are 50 or older. For instance, in 2021, you can improve your IRA contributions by $1,000 and your 401(k) plan contributions by $6,500.

4. Increase Your Donations by Using Bonuses

Consider increasing your retirement contributions with any bonuses or tax refunds you may get. In retirement, you'll be grateful you saved more money.

5. Reconsider Your Contributions Each Year

To make sure you're on track to reach your retirement objectives, it's crucial to reevaluate your retirement contributions every year. Consider raising your donations if you need to give more and lowering them if you contribute too much.

Conclusion

Building a safe retirement depends on regularly contributing to the correct retirement plan. You may choose the best retirement account for you by considering your employer's plan, tax status, and retirement goals. Also, you may make the most of your retirement savings by setting up automatic payments, increasing your contributions over time, taking advantage of catch-up contributions, leveraging windfalls to raise your donations, and reevaluating your contributions yearly. Please don't save for retirement until it's too late; get started to safeguard your financial future.

CHAPTER 7: INVESTING IN LOW-COST INDEX FUNDS TO TAKE ADVANTAGE OF COMPOUND INTEREST OVER TIME

Investing in low-cost index funds is one of the most efficient and reliable methods to increase your money over the long run. You can take advantage of compound interest and create a robust portfolio that will sustain you in the future by selecting the appropriate index fund and investing consistently.

How do Index Funds work?

A mutual fund or exchange-traded fund (ETF) that monitors the performance of a particular index, like the S&P 500 or the Dow Jones Industrial Average, is known as an index fund. An index fund's objective is to deliver returns to investors that closely resemble the performance of the underlying index.

Choosing Index Funds: Why?

The affordability of index funds is one of their key benefits.

Since index funds are passively managed, the fund manager has to put in less effort, which results in cheaper costs for investors. Furthermore, index funds have traditionally outperformed actively managed funds over the long run. This is partly because actively managed funds charge higher fees, which over time, can reduce returns.

How to Choose the Appropriate Index Fund

The cost ratio of an index fund, or the annual fee paid by investors, is an essential factor to consider when selecting an index fund. To guarantee you're not overpaying in fees, look for funds with cost ratios of less than 0.20%.

The performance history of the fund should also be taken into account. Consider investing in funds with a history of outperforming their benchmark index over the long run. But, remember that past performance does not guarantee future outcomes, making it crucial to take other criteria, such as a fund's expenditure ratio, into account as well.

Investing with Index Funds: A Guide

You must open a brokerage account with a reputable online broker to invest in index funds. Once your account is set up, you can select the index fund that best suits your investment objectives and risk tolerance. Via your employer's retirement plan or an individual retirement account, you can invest in index funds (IRA).

Even if you only invest a small sum each month, it's crucial to do so on a regular basis. By doing this, you'll have the chance to reap the benefits of compound interest over time and create a concentrated portfolio that will help you in the future.

Investing Advice For Index Funds

1. Complement Your Portfolio

Diversifying your portfolio is crucial by purchasing various index funds that follow multiple indices. Doing this may lower your risk and ensure you are exposed to all industries and asset classes.

2. Avoid timing the market
Trying to time the market by purchasing and selling index funds based on transient market trends might be alluring. However, this is a dangerous tactic and may result in subpar investment returns. Instead, concentrate on your long-term financial objectives and make consistent investments to gain from compound interest over time.

3. Take Your Portfolio's Rebalancing Into Account
Your index fund investments' value will fluctuate over time, which could lead to an unbalanced portfolio. To ensure that you are not overexposed to any asset class, it is crucial to rebalancing your portfolio regularly. By doing this, you may lower your risk and ensure that your portfolio aligns with your financial objectives.

Conclusion

Putting money into low-cost index funds is a dependable and efficient approach to increasing wealth over time. You may take advantage of compound interest and create a solid portfolio that will sustain you in the future by selecting the appropriate index fund, investing frequently, diversifying your holdings, and avoiding market timing. Index funds are an excellent option for long-term wealth accumulation, regardless of your level of experience with investing.

CHAPTER 8: ADDING DIVERSE INVESTMENTS TO A PORTFOLIO TO REDUCE RISK

A crucial tactic for reducing risk and optimizing profits over the long run is portfolio diversification. You can diversify your risk and shield your portfolio from market volatility by investing in various assets, including stocks, bonds, real estate, and alternative investments.

What Makes A Portfolio Diverse?

Because different assets frequently behave differently depending on the state of the market, diversification is crucial. Bonds may perform well during an economic recession, but equities may perform well during economic expansion. By investing in various assets, you can lessen your exposure to any asset class and shield your portfolio against significant losses.

How to Ensure Portfolio Diversity

You must invest in various assets that are not significantly associated with one another to diversify your portfolio. This means you shouldn't select assets that all travel in the same direction simultaneously. For instance, bonds and stocks frequently correlate negatively, which means that when stocks do poorly, bonds usually do well.

Your investment objectives, risk tolerance, and time horizon should all be considered when choosing the assets for your portfolio. For instance, you might want to devote more of your portfolio to equities if you invest for the long term and have a high-risk tolerance. You might save more of your portfolio on bonds or other fixed-income assets if you support for a short time or have a lower risk tolerance.

Investments To Consider By Type

1. Stocks
Stocks, a form of equity investment, signify ownership in a corporation. Compared to other assets, stores tend to be more volatile, but they also have the potential to produce more significant returns in the long run.

2. Bonds
A fixed-income investment, known as a bond, is a loan that an investor makes to a borrower, usually a business or government body. Bonds typically have lower volatility than stocks and generate consistent income through interest payments.

3. Property
Commercial and residential properties and REITs are all included in real estate investments (real estate investment trusts). Rent payments from real estate assets can be a reliable source of regular income, and their value may increase over time.

4. Diverse Investments
Assets like commodities, private equity, and hedge funds are alternative investments. These investments may have more

significant minimum investment requirements and are typically less liquid than traditional investments. Yet, they can benefit from diversification and may perform well under specific market circumstances.

Advice For Increasing Portfolio Diversification

1. Begin small
Start small and expand your portfolio if you're new to investing. As a result, you can become familiar with various asset classes and investment approaches without taking on excessive risk.

2. Think About Asset Allocation
Distributing your portfolio among various asset classes is referred to as asset allocation. Consider consulting a financial professional to identify the best asset allocation for your investing goals and risk tolerance.

3. Rebalance Your Investments
Your investments' values could fluctuate over time, throwing off the balance of your portfolio. To ensure you are not overexposed to any asset class, it is crucial to rebalancing your portfolio regularly.

4. Continue to diversify
Make sure your portfolio is diversified across various asset classes and industries when you add new investments. By doing this, you'll be able to lower your risk and safeguard your portfolio against market turbulence.

Conclusion

A crucial tactic for reducing risk and optimizing profits over the long run is portfolio diversification. Investing in various assets may diversify your risk and shield your portfolio from market volatility. Diversification is a crucial tactic for creating a robust and durable portfolio that will assist you in the future, regardless of your level of investing experience.

CHAPTER 9: KEEPING UP WITH THE MARKET AND ECONOMIC SITUATIONS

Successful investment requires a continuous understanding of economic and financial developments. You can make better investing selections and adjust your strategy to shifting market conditions by staying current on news and events. Here are some pointers on how to keep up with economic and market movements.

1. Read business news

Reading financial news is one of the important ways to stay informed about market movements and economic situations. Financial information is available from various sources, such as newspapers, periodicals, and websites. The Wall Street Journal, Bloomberg, and CNBC are a few well-liked financial news sources. Regularly reading financial news lets, you keep up with the most recent changes in the stock market, interest rates, and other important economic indicators.

2. Monitor market indicators

Market indices like the Dow Jones Industrial Average and the S&P 500 helped observe broad market patterns. These indexes give you a picture of the market's activity and can be used to spot trends and business possibilities. To keep you updated about the state of the market, many financial news outlets regularly update market indices.

3. Utilize tools for investing

You can stay informed about market trends and economic situations with the aid of a variety of investment instruments. For instance, stock screening software can help you find prospective investing possibilities based on predetermined standards like market capitalization or price-to-earnings ratio. To assess the success of your investments and spot trends over time, you can also use portfolio tracking tools.

4. Participate in investor conferences.

Keeping up with market trends and economic situations can be done by attending investment conferences. These gatherings frequently offer keynote speakers, panel discussions, and networking opportunities. You may interact with other investors, learn about cutting-edge investment techniques, and gain knowledge from subject-matter experts.

5. Use social media

Staying informed about market trends and economic situations can be done using social media sites like Twitter and LinkedIn. You can find a lot of financial news sources and investment experts on social media, and they frequently give insights and analyses that might aid in your decision-making.

6. Get advice from financial advisors

Working with a financial advisor can be a helpful method to keep up with the market and economic developments. A financial advisor can offer you individualized investing guidance based on your unique goals and risk tolerance. Also, they may assist you in keeping abreast of economic and market changes so that you can modify your investing strategy as necessary.

7. Examine Financial Data

Economic statistics like GDP growth, inflation, and unemployment can give important insights into the state of the economy. You can see patterns and possible investment opportunities by researching economic data. You can obtain economic data from various financial news sources and investment tools, keeping you updated about important trends.

Conclusion

Successful investment requires staying knowledgeable about market trends and macroeconomic situations. You may keep current on the most recent developments and make more informed investing decisions by reading financial news, watching market indices, using investment tools, attending investor conferences, following social media, talking with financial experts, and evaluating economic data. Although it's crucial to maintain discipline and adhere to your investment strategy, being informed may also help you spot opportunities and steer clear of traps.

CHAPTER 10: REFRAINING FROM IMPULSIVE PURCHASES AND MAINTAINING A CONTROLLED BUDGET

Managing your expenditure is one of the significant obstacles to obtaining financial stability and accumulating wealth. Your financial goals can be derailed by impulsive purchases, excessive spending, and a lack of discipline, resulting in a vicious cycle of debt and worry. Yet, you can take charge of your money and move closer to your long-term objectives by avoiding impulse buys and adhering to a disciplined spending plan.

1. Establish a Budget

Establishing a budget is the first step in preventing impulsive purchases and maintaining a disciplined spending plan. A budget is a plan for your income and expenses that lets you keep tabs on your spending and make wise financial decisions. Include your monthly income, fixed costs like utilities, insurance, rent or mortgage payments, and rent or mortgage payments. Next, set aside a percentage of your salary for savings and luxuries like entertainment and dining out. Track your spending and adjust your expenses to stay within your budget.

2. Resist being tempted

Temptation is one of the most significant barriers to resisting impulsive purchases. It can be challenging to control the impulse to spend money, whether from a sale at your favorite store, a bright commercial, or peer pressure to keep up with peers. Limit your exposure to marketing and advertising, unsubscribe from promotional emails, and refrain from window shopping or perusing online stores when you don't need to purchase to prevent temptation. To lessen the likelihood of impulsive purchases, consider taking your credit cards out of your wallet or turning off one-click purchasing possibilities.

3. Make Smart Purchases.

Shopping with a goal is another technique to prevent impulsive purchases. Before purchasing, consider if you need the item and whether it fits within your spending plan and long-term financial objectives. If you want enough time to decide whether the expense is required, think about waiting 24 hours before purchasing. Planning your shopping visits and making a list of the things you need to buy will help you resist the urge to buy something you don't need.

4. Take Opportunity Cost into Account

To avoid impulsive purchases, think about the opportunity cost. When you make an impulsive purchase, you forfeit the chance to put that money to work for you by investing it or saving it. Consider whether the item is worth sacrificing your long-term financial goals before you make a purchase. Think about how it will affect your finances and whether saving or investing that money for the future would be wiser.

5. Exercise self-control

And finally, self-control is necessary to follow a disciplined spending strategy. This entails establishing boundaries for oneself, establishing a schedule, and acting consistently. Discover methods to treat yourself to a tiny indulgence or to recognize your accomplishments as a reward for staying within your budget. Be in the Company of people who will help you stay accountable and support your financial goals. And keep in mind that developing a habit like a self-discipline requires time and repetition, so have patience and keep your eyes on your objectives.

Conclusion

For financial stability and wealth creation, avoiding impulsive purchases and maintaining a strict budget are crucial. You may take charge of your money and move closer to your long-term goals by creating a budget, resisting temptation, shopping with a purpose, weighing the opportunity cost, and exercising self-control. Good spending habits require time and effort, but financial security and independence benefits make an effort worthwhile.

CHAPTER 11: USING TECHNOLOGY AND AUTOMATION TO REDUCE LABOR COSTS AND INCREASE PRODUCTIVITY

Time is a crucial resource in today's fast-paced world, and it often converts into financial savings. There are many methods to simplify our everyday duties and routines thanks to technological and automated advances, which can make us more productive, efficient, and ultimately more cost-effective. By saving us time, lowering our expenses, and raising our earning potential, harnessing the power of technology and automation can assist us in reaching our financial objectives.

1. Streamline Your Finances

Automating your finances is among the simplest and most efficient methods to save time and money. You may prevent late fees and penalties and ensure you're consistently contributing to your savings objectives by automating your bills and savings. Set up automatic transfers to your savings and investment accounts and monthly payments for your expenses, including rent, electricity, and credit card balances. Without requiring frequent manual intervention, this can assist you in maintaining your financial goals.

2. Monitor Your Spending Using Apps and Tools

Using tools and applications to keep track of your spending is another way to leverage technology to save time and money. Many apps that can help you keep tabs on your spending, create financial objectives, and track your success are free or at a minimal fee. This might assist you in locating potential areas of overspending so that you can adapt your budget appropriately.

3. Save time and money by shopping online

Internet shopping has grown in popularity over the past few years, and for good reason. Shopping online can save you time and money by removing the need to drive to real places, compare prices, and deal with crowds. You can save money on your purchases by taking advantage of the discounts, free shipping, and other promotions that online shops frequently provide.

4. Use online coupons and discount codes

Using electronic coupons and discount codes is another way to reduce costs while purchasing online. For discounts, free delivery, and other benefits, many retailers provide coupons and discount codes that can be redeemed at the checkout. These codes can be found on social media, coupon websites, and retailer newsletters, among other places.

5. Automate your portfolio of investments

Although it can take a lot of time and effort, investing is crucial in accumulating wealth. Automating your investment portfolio is one method to make investing more straightforward and effective. Numerous investment platforms have automatic investment options, enabling you to make recurring contributions to your accounts.

6. Make use of chatbots and virtual assistants

In recent years, virtual assistants and chatbots have grown in popularity, and for a good reason. By managing typical chores like appointment scheduling, reminders, and shared queries, these apps can help you automate jobs and save time. Doing this may free up time for more important activities, like developing your business or spending time with your loved ones.

Conclusion

Using technology and automation can enable you to save time and money while achieving your financial objectives. You may simplify your everyday duties and routines and concentrate on what matters most by automating your finances, using apps and tools to track your costs, buying online, using digital discounts and promo codes, automating your investment portfolio, and employing virtual assistants and chatbots. Always remember that technology and automation are just tools, and it is up to you to use them in a way consistent with your beliefs and financial objectives. With some forethought and work, you can use technology to save time and money and achieve financial freedom.

CHAPTER 12: CREATING A SIDE BUSINESS OR FREELANCING GIG TO BOOST YOUR INCOME

Many Millennial's seek ways to boost their income due to the rising cost of living and the mounting pressure to save for retirement. Creating a side business or finding freelance employment that can generate a reliable source of additional money is a standard answer. Selling products or services online or taking on freelance work in a particular industry are also examples of side hustles. Creating a side business or engaging in freelance work can be a terrific way to boost your income while gaining valuable experience and mastering new skills.

1. Determine Your Talents and Skills

Identifying your abilities and talents is the first step in creating a successful side business or freelancing project. Think about your strengths and your interests. Do you have a pastime or interest that could be developed into a successful business? Do you possess any marketable skills acquired through employment or education? Once you've determined your areas of expertise, you may start looking for chances to start a side business or do freelance work.

2. Market research

Once you've determined your strengths, conducting market research is critical to find prospects for a side business or freelance employment. Search for market gaps where your abilities can be helpful, and research the goods and services similar companies or people provide. Use online groups, forums, and social media to learn what people want and are willing to pay for.

3. Create a Strategy

Now that you know the market and the potential, it's time to create a strategy for your side business or freelance work. Be sure to decide on your product or service, marketing plan, and pricing strategy. Make a realistic timeline and budget for starting your side business or freelance work after considering the time and resources you'll need to invest in it.

4. Create a Brand

It would help if you built a brand for your side business or freelance employment to succeed. Create a name, logo, and website that accurately represent your good or service. You should also have a unified brand voice and visual style for your marketing collateral. Build your audience, market your brand via social media, blogs, and other platforms, and interact with your clients to foster a sense of loyalty and trust.

5. Network and Work Together

Networking and collaboration can be beneficial when starting a side business or doing freelance work. Forge connections with other experts in your field, participate in online communities and attend industry events to learn about the market. Seek ways to work with other companies or people to increase your reach and develop your brand.

6. Handle Your Resources and Time

While starting a side business or doing freelance work, time management and resource management is crucial. To prevent burnout, balancing your side business and other obligations, such as your employment or family, is critical. Use tools like calendars and project management software to keep organized and prioritize your work. It would help if you were willing to delegate or outsource tasks you don't have time to do.

Conclusion

Creating a side business or engaging in freelance work can be an excellent way to boost your income and acquire the necessary experience and abilities. You can build a successful side business or freelance gig that supports your financial objectives and advances your professional development by identifying your skills and talents, researching the market, developing a plan, developing a brand, networking, working with others, and managing your time and resources. Just keep in mind that creating a side business or doing freelance work takes time, effort, and attention, but with the correct attitude and approach, it can be a fulfilling and profitable undertaking.

CHAPTER 13: SALARY AND BENEFIT NEGOTIATIONS TO INCREASE EARNING POTENTIAL

Negotiating your wage and benefits can be critical in achieving financial success in today's competitive employment market. Even with this, many Millennial's could feel awkward or underprepared while negotiating their pay package. Millennial's may optimize their earning potential and ensure future financial security by learning the value of negotiating and adopting a communication plan.

Researching your position and the going rates in your field is the first step in negotiating your salary and perks. Internet resources, such as salary calculators and industry reports, can be a great source of information about the average pay range for your job title and experience level. Also, networking with industry experts will help you learn important details about current recruiting and wage trends.

Developing a clear and concise message for negotiation is crucial once you fully grasp your market value. This can involve showcasing your abilities, knowledge, and accomplishments that make you a valued asset to the business. Also, you might want to consider going over specific objectives or goals for your job, like chances for advancement or professional development.

Throughout the bargaining process, keeping your communications with your employer professional and upbeat is critical. A threat to leave the Company or a request might hurt your connection with your employer and restrict your prospects for advancement in the future. Instead, think of bargaining as a chance to work with your Company to devise a win-win solution.

It's crucial to negotiate your wage and the benefits package your employer is willing to supply. Healthcare, retirement plans, and additional benefits like flexible scheduling or tuition assistance may fall under this category. You may plan for your financial future and bargain for the finest perks by being fully aware of the scope of your pay package.

In the end, pay and benefits negotiations necessitate a blend of self-assurance, thorough study, and tactful communication. You can optimize your earning potential and achieve financial security by going into negotiations knowing precisely what your market value and professional objectives are. With proper planning and communication, Millennial's can take charge of their financial destiny and achieve the pay they deserve.

CHAPTER 14:
USING EMPLOYER-SPONSORED RETIREMENT PLANS AND INVESTMENT MATCHING SCHEMES

One of the most significant financial objectives for everyone, including Millennial's, is saving for retirement. Happily, many firms have retirement plans, like 401(k)s, that let workers keep for their later years through pre-tax contributions that can grow tax-free until withdrawal. Some businesses might also provide matching grants, considerably increasing retirement savings.

Employer-sponsored retirement plans and investment matching programs should be a key priority for Millennial's who want to secure their financial future. Here are some pointers to help you make the most of these apps' advantages:

1. Comprehend your employer's retirement plan: You must be aware of how it operates before you can begin contributing to it. Review the plan papers and contact your human resources office to fully comprehend the contribution caps, investment choices, and any matching contributions your Company might make.

2. Make a minimum contribution to qualify for the Company match: Many employers will match your contributions to a particular percentage of your pay. As the Company match is essentially free money that can considerably increase your retirement savings, making at least the minimum required contribution is crucial to earning the entire workplace match.

3. Gradually raise your contribution rate: Don't panic if you can't afford to make the maximum contribution to your employer's retirement plan immediately. As your income rises or your costs decline, increase your contribution rate gradually from the first comfortable level.

4. Take into account the Roth option. A Roth option is a retirement plan provided by your Company that enables you to contribute after-tax dollars that can grow tax-free and be withdrawn tax-free in retirement. This can be a fantastic alternative for Millennial's who anticipate being in a higher tax band in retirement than they are today.

5. Diversify your investments: To reduce risk and increase profits, you should diversify your retirement investments. Most employer-sponsored retirement plans provide a range of investment choices, such as target date and mutual funds. Review the investing alternatives and select a variety of investments that fit your risk profile and long-term objectives.

6. Continually review and tweak your contributions: To ensure you are on pace to reach your retirement objectives, it is a good idea to check your retirement contributions routinely. To stay on pace, think about changing your contribution rate or investment mix.

7. Avoid early withdrawals: In general, it's not a good idea to take money out of your retirement account before you're 59 1/2 years old because you might have to pay taxes and penalties for doing so.

Instead, consider other ways to access money, including setting up an emergency fund or getting a low-interest loan.

In conclusion, utilizing employer-sponsored retirement plans and investment matching programs can be an effective instrument for securing the future of your finances. You can position yourself for a comfortable retirement by understanding your employer's retirement plan, making enough payments to qualify for the employer match, increasing your contributions over time, diversifying your investments, and frequent monitoring and modifying your contributions.

CHAPTER 15: MAKING PREPARATIONS FOR SIGNIFICANT LIFE EVENTS LIKE PROPERTY PURCHASES AND FAMILY FORMATION

Important life milestones like purchasing a home, beginning a family, or going to college can be thrilling, but they can also be expensive. To prevent financial stress and maintain financial stability, preparing in advance for these eventualities is crucial.

Setting financial objectives is one of the first steps in preparing for significant life events. Finding out how much money is required, when it is needed, and how it will be supported are all included in this. For instance, saving a specified sum of money over a predetermined time may be necessary for a down payment on a House. Individuals can plan to accomplish their financial goals and stay on course by defining precise goals in this area.

Budgeting is a key component of planning for significant life events. To do this, make a spending plan that prioritizes savings and covers all necessary costs. People can free up money toward their financial objectives by keeping track of their expenditures and finding places to cut back.

It might be challenging to save for significant life events, but there are many ways to improve savings. Setting up automated savings transfers is one typical tactic. People can routinely increase their savings without actively thinking about it by transferring the money into a designated account each month.

Using tax-advantaged savings accounts, such as a 529 plan for educational costs or a Health Savings Account (HSA) for medical expenses, can also help to maximize savings and lower taxes. These accounts provide tax advantages that can boost savings and lower the cost of significant life events.

It's crucial to consider how your choices may affect your financial objectives in the long run when preparing for significant life events. A degree that may not lead to a high-paying career or taking on excessive debt to buy a home, for instance, can have a detrimental effect on long-term financial security. Major life events can have long-term effects that should be considered to help people make decisions that align with their financial objectives.

Financial strategies should be reviewed and modified as circumstances change. For instance, unanticipated costs or variations in income could necessitate a reevaluation of financial objectives and plans. Individuals can stay on track and make any adjustments by periodically evaluating their financial goals.

In conclusion, preparation for significant life events is crucial for preserving financial stability and realizing financial objectives. People can plan for these occurrences and reduce financial stress by making precise objectives, budgeting, and savings priorities. To maximize savings and maintain financial stability over the long term, taking advantage of tax-advantaged savings accounts and thinking about the long-term effects of significant life events can also be helpful. People can realize their desires and safeguard their financial future with careful planning and focusing on economic objectives.

CHAPTER 16:
GETTING GUIDANCE
AND TRAINING TO
INCREASE FINANCIAL
LITERACY

Making wise and prudent financial decisions starts with financial literacy. Yet, many people need more information and abilities to manage their funds efficiently. To increase financial literacy and reach financial objectives, seeking financial guidance and instruction can be helpful.

Identifying your areas of need is one of the first steps in getting financial assistance and education. This can involve investing, planning for retirement, managing debt, and creating a budget. You can look for tools to help you increase your financial literacy once you've determined the areas in which you require assistance.

Workshops and seminars held in the community are one option for financial education. Various economic issues are covered at these meetings, frequently hosted by financial experts. Attending these programs can give you insightful knowledge about financial planning techniques and introduce you to others who share your interest in enhancing their financial literacy.

Online classes and tutorials are other sources for financial education. Online sources come in many forms, including webinars, podcasts, and videos. These materials offer quick and easy ways to learn about economic subjects and may be accessed anytime and anywhere.

Working with a financial advisor or planner can be beneficial in addition to seeking education and resources. A financial advisor can give you individualized advice on financial planning techniques and assist you in creating a strategy to reach your financial objectives. Financial advisors can assist you in managing your account and offer insightful advice on effective investment methods.

Engaging with a credible and knowledgeable expert while seeking financial assistance is crucial. Find financial advisors who have a license from and are registered with regulatory bodies like the Securities and Exchange Commission (SEC) or the Financial Industry Regulatory Authority (FINRA). Also, you can look for reviews and ratings online or get recommendations from family and friends.

Becoming more financially literate is a continuous process, so keeping up with current financial trends and tactics is critical. People can make wise financial decisions and reach long-term financial objectives by seeking financial education and counseling.

Finally, obtaining financial education and assistance is a critical first step in raising financial literacy and reaching financial objectives. Working with a financial advisor, attending community programs, and using online resources can all help you gain the necessary knowledge and direction on financial planning techniques. People can make educated judgments and lay a solid basis for long-term financial stability by investing in financial education and seeking reliable advisors.

CHAPTER 17: AVOIDING HIGH-INTEREST DEBT, SUCH AS CREDIT CARD DEBT

A significant barrier to obtaining financial stability might be high-interest debt, such as credit card debt. While particular debt—such as a mortgage or student loan—may be required to reach specific objectives, high-interest debt can quickly mount and strain your budget. A crucial first step to becoming financially successful is avoiding high-interest loans.

Understanding your financial condition is the first step in avoiding high-interest debt. This includes being aware of your earnings, outgoings, and debts. You can create a budget to manage your costs and prevent taking on high-interest debt after you have a clear picture of your resources.

The wise use of credit cards is one of the best methods to avoid high-interest debt. Credit cards can be a valuable financial tool when used appropriately, but when misused, they can result in high-interest debt. Utilizing credit cards for necessary expenditures and making total monthly payments is crucial. This can assist you in avoiding interest fees and preserving a high credit score.

It's crucial to take action to pay off high-interest debt if you currently have it to do so as soon as feasible. Focusing on paying off debts with the highest interest rates first is one tactic. This can help you pay off debt more quickly and lower the overall interest you pay.

To avoid high-interest debt, you can also start an emergency fund. In the event of unforeseen needs, having an emergency fund can prevent you from utilizing credit cards or taking out loans. You may avoid piling up high-interest debt and keep your financial security by keeping a cushion of reserves.

It's also crucial to exercise caution when considering taking on loans or other types of debt. It's critical to consider the fees and interest rates related to the loan before applying for one. The loan's terms, such as the time frame for repayment and any fines associated with late or missed payments, should also be considered.

Maintaining a high credit score and avoiding high-interest loans are crucial. You may be eligible for loans and credit cards with cheaper interest rates if you have a high credit score, ultimately saving you money. It's critical to pay your payments on time, keep your credit card balances low, and refrain from opening many new credit accounts if you want to keep your credit score high.

In conclusion, staying away from debt with a high-interest rate is a crucial first step toward financial stability. People can avoid raising debt that could strain their finances by using credit cards properly, paying off high-interest debt, saving for emergencies, and being cautious when considering loans. Keeping a high credit score is also crucial because it might make you eligible for loans and credit cards with lower interest rates. Anyone can achieve long-term financial success by taking these measures to avoid high-interest loans.

CHAPTER 18: CONCENTRATING ON LONG-TERM OBJECTIVES WHILE AVOIDING QUICK-RICHES SCHEMES

The secret to financial success for Millennial's may lie in concentrating on long-term objectives and avoiding get-rich-quick schemes. Investing in long-term goals can help develop wealth over time and ensure a secure financial future, despite the temptation to try and earn a fast profit.

Here are some pointers for concentrating on long-term objectives while avoiding quick-rich schemes:

1. Specify your long-term financial objectives: The first step is to identify your long-term financial objectives. This can involve launching a business, paying off debt, investing for retirement, or purchasing a property. You can plan to accomplish your goals once you've established them.

2. Make a budget. A budget can keep you focused on your long-term objectives. You can ensure that you are living within your

means and setting aside money for your goals by understanding how much money you have coming in and going out each month.

3. Have a varied portfolio of investments: Doing so can help you lower risk and accumulate wealth over time. Consider investing in various assets, such as stocks, bonds, and real estate, instead of just one store or industry.

4. Avoid programs that promise to make you wealthy soon. Numerous frauds out there make this claim. Beware of day trading, multilevel marketing, and pyramid schemes, among others, that seem too good to be true. Instead, concentrate on long-term investing.

5. Continue on course: Making long-term investments requires staying the course through market ups and downs. As the market dips, resist the urge to sell out of panic because you can miss out on good possibilities. Stay the course and have faith in your investment strategy instead.

6. Educate yourself: Avoiding get-rich-quick schemes and making wise investing selections require education. To understand more about investing and money, read books, attend seminars, and speak with financial advisors.

7. Have patience: Creating wealth requires time, so don't anticipate immediate returns. You can create a solid financial foundation and attain financial success over time by remaining focused on your long-term objectives and rejecting get-rich-quick schemes.

In conclusion, Millennial's must reject get-rich-quick schemes and concentrate on long-term goals to succeed financially. You may lay a strong foundation and realize your financial goals by setting goals, making a budget, investing in a diversified portfolio, staying the course, being patient, and avoiding scams.

CHAPTER 19: KEEPING A BALANCED WORK-LIFE SCHEDULE TO PREVENT BURNOUT AND BOOST PRODUCTIVITY

Maintaining a healthy work-life balance is crucial for both personal and professional well-being. It lets people divide their time between several facets, such as jobs, family, hobbies, and self-care. Striking the correct balance can be difficult, particularly in today's hectic and demanding workplace. To minimize burnout and boost productivity, it is crucial to prioritize this area of one's life.

Setting up distinct boundaries between work and personal time is one of the first steps in achieving a healthy work-life balance. Setting aside time for family, friends, interests, and self-care is crucial. Work should not interfere with these pursuits. This can be accomplished by creating a schedule that distinguishes between work and personal time and following it as closely as possible.

Managing your workload and setting reasonable expectations is crucial to maintain a healthy work-life balance. Prioritizing work based on relevance and urgency is vital to prevent taking on more than one can handle. Individuals may be able to avoid feeling pressured and overloaded as a result.

Employers can help to encourage work-life balance in a number of ways. Offering flexible work options, including telecommuting or flexible scheduling, and encouraging staff to take time off as needed might accomplish this. This can improve job satisfaction and productivity while lowering stress and burnout.

Another crucial component of preserving a healthy work-life balance is self-care. This can involve exercising or playing sports, getting enough sleep, eating a balanced diet, and engaging in mindfulness or meditation. These exercises can aid people in managing their stress and enhancing their general well-being.

Also, avoiding using technology and engaging in activities linked to your job during downtime is crucial. As a result, people may experience less tension and more relaxation, which will help them unwind and be more productive when they return to work.

Finally, it's critical to remember that finding a healthy work-life balance is a process that calls for continuous effort and focus. That is not an isolated incident nor an easy repair. To ensure they are using their time and energy wisely, people must be aware of their priorities and make changes as necessary.

In conclusion, maintaining a healthy work-life balance is crucial for both personal and professional well-being. To do this, people must clearly define the lines between work and personal time, manage their workload, prioritize self-care, and avoid engaging in work-related activities at home. Companies can help employees achieve a healthy work-life balance by providing flexible scheduling options and supporting time off when necessary. Finding a healthy work-life balance is ongoing and demands constant effort and focus, but the rewards are enormous, including improved productivity, job satisfaction, and general

KAITLIN HENDERSON

well-being.

CHAPTER 20: CONSIDERING NON-TRADITIONAL INVESTMENT OPTIONS LIKE REAL ESTATE OR CRYPTOCURRENCIES.

While traditional options like stocks, bonds, and mutual funds are the most popular, investing has always been crucial to accumulating wealth. Many Millennial's are now looking into alternative options like real estate and cryptocurrency. The potential rewards from these alternative investment opportunities are higher, but the risks are also higher.

For decades, real estate has been a well-liked investment choice. A real estate is still an attractive option for Millennial's trying to accumulate money. One of the main benefits of real estate is that it generates passive income through rent payments, which can be used to either supplement or replace mortgage payments. Real estate is a tangible asset that can increase in value over time, offering the possibility of significant monetary gains. But, investing in real estate necessitates a substantial initial outlay of cash, and ongoing costs such as property taxes, insurance, and maintenance must be considered.

Cryptocurrency is another alternative investment option that has grown in popularity recently. Cryptocurrencies like Bitcoin, Ethereum, and Litecoin have the potential to generate huge profits, but they also carry a sizable amount of risk due to their high volatility. Because there is no regulation or monitoring and the value of cryptocurrencies can vary quickly, they should only be used as speculative investments. Also, there is a chance that your cash could be lost due to fraud and security flaws.

Evaluating your risk tolerance and investment objectives before considering alternative options is critical. Before investing your money, conducting extensive study and exercising due diligence is crucial. Partnering with a financial advisor or investing specialist can help you understand the complex world of alternative investments and make informed selections.

Diversifying your financial portfolio is crucial, regardless of whether you select conventional or alternative investing possibilities. By distributing your investment over various asset types and investment vehicles, diversification helps reduce risk. You may ensure that your investment results are independent of any investment by maintaining a well-diversified portfolio.

As a result, while alternative investment possibilities like real estate and cryptocurrencies may have the potential to yield more significant returns, they also carry greater risks. Before considering alternative investments, assessing your risk tolerance and investing objectives is essential.

You should also conduct your research and consult a financial counselor. To reduce risk and guarantee that your investment returns are not unduly dependent on any one investment, it is also crucial to diversify your portfolio of assets.

CONCLUSION.

Millennial's are frequently called the "lost generation" in personal finance because they comprise most of the workforce. Many people have had difficulty establishing themselves in the post-recession economy as a result of their heavy school debt, stagnating salaries, and precarious employment. This only sometimes means that hope is lost for Millennial's who want to accumulate wealth over time.

In truth, even in financial difficulties, Millennial's can employ a few basic tactics to accumulate wealth quietly. These tactics include creating a sound financial plan, spending money on their education and professional growth, and exercising good judgment when investing and saving.

Creating a thorough financial plan is one of Millennial's' most crucial actions to increase their wealth. A budget that represents their priorities for spending, debt management plans, and savings accumulation tactics should all be included in this plan. It should also have goals for both short- and long-term financial success.

Millennial's may stay on track toward their financial objectives and avoid common mistakes that might sabotage their success by taking the time to build a plan and routinely track their progress.

Investing in one's education and professional growth is another crucial option for Millennial's. This could be going back to school for a graduate degree, getting a professional certification, looking for skills-building and training opportunities, or just keeping up with current market trends and best practices. Millennial's may position themselves for higher-paying employment and longer-term financial security by investing in their knowledge and abilities.

Millennial's should make wise choices that will enable them to accumulate money over time when saving and investing. This could entail setting aside retirement savings through an IRA or 401(k), investing in exchange-traded funds (ETFs) and low-cost index funds, or setting up an emergency fund to support you through tough financial times. Millennial's may establish the framework for long-term financial security and success by making these kinds of wise investments.

And last, Millennial's must have a disciplined and patient approach to accumulating wealth. Although it is not a quick or straightforward process, individuals prepared to put in the time and work can become wealthy gradually. Millennial's may lay a solid foundation for financial success by adhering to their financial plan, continuing to invest in themselves and their professions, and making prudent decisions regarding saving and investing.

In conclusion, Millennial's who wish to accumulate wealth gradually can accomplish it by implementing a few crucial tactics. Millennial's can build long-term financial security and achieve their financial goals over time by creating a sound financial plan, making an investment in their education and career development, making wise choices when it comes to saving and investing, and upholding a mindset of patience and discipline. Even though it may not always be simple, achieving financial success is possible for those prepared to work and remain dedicated to their objectives.